NATURE AND CULTURE

FOREIGN LANGUAGES PRESS

First Edition 2004

ISBN 7-119-03401-4
©Foreign Languages Press, Beijing, China, 2004
Published by Foreign Languages Press
24 Baiwanzhuang Road, Beijing 100037, China
Website: http://www.flp.com.cn
E-mail Addresses: Info@flp.com.cn
Sales@flp.com.cn
Distributed by China International Book Trading Corporation
35 Chegongzhuang Xilu, Beijing 100044, China
P.O. Box 399, Beijing, China

Printed in the People's Republic of China

Preface

As a world-renowned country with an ancient civilization, China boasts a wealth of cultural relics and historical sites, such as the ten thousand-li Great Wall, the Imperial Palace in Beijing, the Dunhuang Grottoes, and the Potala Palace in Lhasa. In particular, the Great Wall has been called one of the Wonders of the World.

It has become the common responsibility of all mankind to preserve the natural and cultural wealth created by our ancestors. Moreover, people are becoming more aware of the importance of looking after these priceless treasures so that we can hand them down to later generations. Over the past few decades, people throughout the world have made efforts to various degrees to preserve their cultural and natural heritages. In the third century BC, the Ramses Dynasty in Egypt established a mouseion, from which the English word "museum" is derived, in the imperial palace in Alexandria. It was a special temple for housing valuable cultural relics. The pyramids of Egypt and ancient structures of many other countries in the world have been preserved by the authorities. China boasts a collection of inscriptions on bones and tortoise shells which date from the Shang Dynasty (18th-11th centuries BC). In the Zhou Dynasty (C. 1100-221 BC), a great number of famous articles and valuables were kept in special collection rooms, and registered in the *Records*. Besides collecting valuable cultural relics, the local authorities in China throughout history made efforts to preserve special palaces, cemeteries and ancestral temples, mountains, rivers, trees, historical sites, gardens and ponds. There was also a solid folk tradition of preserving public buildings, ancestral temples and guild halls, irrigation works, mountains, rivers and trees through local rules and popular conventions. The details of such preservation measures were inscribed on tablets.

With the development of communications, information transmission and tourism, people have become more aware of the importance of protecting their cultural and natural heritages, especially from damage resulting from industrialization in the modern era. Therefore, some experts, scholars and far-sighted personages of various countries have made appeals for joint protection of the common wealth of mankind, and passed the Athens Charter, Venice Charter, Washington Charter, Lausanne Charter, the Europe and American conventions to preserve archaeological and historical heritages, the Suggestions on the Protection of the Landscape and the Styles, Features and Characteristics of Relics of the United Nations Educational, Scientific and Cultural Organization (UNESCO), etc. To further strengthen the protection and management of cultural relics, and get national governments to pay more attention and extend more support to these endeavors, the Convention on the Protection of the World's Cultural and Natural Heritages was adopted at the 17th UNESCO Conference in Paris in November 1972, explicitly regulating the definition and standards of the world's cultural and natural heritage sites, and setting the guiding principle of its implementation, which is a standard international document of far-reaching influence promulgated and carried out by UNESCO throughout the world. One of its main tasks is to determine items of cultural and natural heritage of prominent significance and universal value generally accepted by the whole world, and list them in the World Heritage List as the common heritage of mankind, to promote cooperation and mutual support among people of all countries and ethnic groups, and make active contributions to the protection of this heritage.

To guarantee that all the regulations of the Heritage Convention win the support and cooperation of all countries, the World Heritage Committee (WHC), an organization of international cooperation between governments was founded in 1976, supported by 21 of the signatory states to the Convention on the Protection of the World's Cultural and Natural Heritage. The organization's headquarters is the UNESCO Center for the Protection of the World Heritage. The WHC holds a meeting every year, to mainly engage in three items of work: First, discussing and determining the projects to be proposed for inclusion in the World Heritage List and submitting them to the representative conferences of the signatory states for adoption and promulgation. Second, supervising the World Heritage Fund, and examining and approving the financial and technical support put forward by the signatory states. The fund is composed of one percent of the regular membership dues of UNESCO member states and voluntary contributions from the governments of the signatory states and other organizations and individuals. Despite its small size, the fund has played an active role in promoting the protection of some important items of cultural and natural heritage in many countries, especially the developing countries and underdeveloped regions. Third, monitoring the protection and management of the cultural and natural heritage projects listed in the World Heritage List.

To improve the quality of the work of protection, evaluation, survey and technical support, UNESCO and the WHC consult the International Council on Monuments and Sites (ICOMOS), International Union for the Protection of Nature and Natural Resources (IUCN), and the International Center for the Study of the Preservation and Restoration of Cultural Property (ICCROM), which assist with research and publicity work, as well as offering the services of experts.

Definitions of cultural heritage:

1. Cultural relics: Viewed from the historic, artistic or scientific angle, the buildings, sculptures and paintings of prominent and universal value, components and structures of archaeological significance, inscriptions, caves, residential areas and various combinations of the above.

2. Buildings: Viewed from the historic, artistic or scientific angle, independent or associated buildings of prominent and universal value due to their style, structure or position in the landscape.

3. Ruins: Viewed from the historic, aesthetic, ethnological or anthropological angle, artificial projects or common masterpieces of man and nature, and archaeological ruins of prominent and universal value.

Evaluation standards for cultural heritage sites:

1. Masterwork representing a unique achievement or creative talent.

2. Work that has had a significant influence on the development of architecture, urban construction or landscape designs during some period or in some cultural region in the world.

3. Work that can offer a unique or at least special evidence for a lost civilization or cultural tradition.

4. Work that shows one or several important stages of human history as an example of the masterwork of a kind of building or landscape.

5. Vulnerable site as an example of the human residential area or usable land of one or more cultural traditions, especially if an irreversible change threatens.

6. Material object of special universal significance, directly or substantially associated with modern current traditional ideas, beliefs or literary or artistic works. (According to experts, this article can be considered as a standard for a cultural heritage site listed in the World Heritage List only under some special situation or when it is jointly considered with other standards.)

Definition of natural heritage:

1. Viewed from the aesthetic or scientific angle, geological or biological structures of prominent and universal value or the natural features of similar structures.

2. Viewed from the scientific or protection angle, geological or natural geographical features of prominent and universal value, and explicitly designated habitats of endangered species of animals and plants.

3. Viewed from the scientific or natural aesthetic angle, natural scenic spots of prominent and universal value, or explicitly designated nature reserves.

Evaluation standards for natural heritage sites:

1. Outstanding examples of the important stages of the history of global evolution.

2. Important phenomena occurring during the process of geological or biological evolution, and important examples of the relations between man and the natural environment.

3. Unique, rare or ingenious natural phenomena or topographic features, or locations of rare natural beauty.

4. Habitats of rare or endangered animals or plants.

In addition, the WHC may list seriously threatened or endangered sites of cultural and natural heritage in the World Heritage List so as to adopt emergency measures to save and protect them after investigations and discussions by experts.

Always attaching great importance to the protection of items of cultural and natural heritage, the government of the People's Republic of China actively takes part in activities designed to protect the world's cultural and natural heritages carried out by UNESCO and the CWH. In November 1985, at the proposal of relevant experts, scholars and members of the Chinese People's Political Consultative Conference (CPPCC), the Standing Committee of the National People's Congress gave China approval to become one of the signatory states to the Convention on the Protection of the World's Cultural and Natural Heritages of UNESCO. In 1986, China requested that the Great Wall, the Imperial Palace in Beijing, the relics of Peking Man at Zhoukoudian, the Mogao Grottoes at Dunhuang, the Mausoleum of the First Qin Emperor and the terracotta army and Mount Taishan be included in the World Heritages List. The request was approved by the WHC in 1987, after careful examinations. China was elected one of the members of the WHC at the Eighth Conference of the Signatory States to the Convention on the Protection of the World's Cultural and Natural Heritages in October 1991. China's representative was elected vice-president of the committee at the 16th and 17th conferences of the WHC in 1992 and December 1993, respectively.

The culture and traditions of the Chinese nation have had an unbroken history of several thousand years. As a country composed of many ethnic groups since ancient times, China has created a brilliant multi-ethnic culture in the process of its long historical development, represented by many masterpieces, such as the Potala Palace and the Chengde Mountain Resort and Its Outlying Temples. The murals and painted sculptures in the Mogao Caves at Dunhuang, and the Mausoleum of the First Qin Emperor and his terracotta army are also world-famous cultural treasures. In the realm of natural heritage, scenic areas such as those of Jiuzhaigou and Wulingyuan are characterized by unique geological and topographical features, animals and plants, and beautiful scenery. Many sites with both natural and cultural heritage features, including Taishan, Wuyi and Emei mountains, and the Leshan Giant Buddha Scenic Area, reflect the integration of China's long history and culture with its natural environment, which is rarely seen in other countries. Meanwhile, the cultural scenic spot of Mount Lushan has been approved for putting on the List as "an ingenious work integrating a beautiful natural environment with excellent human artistry."

As a contribution to protecting, studying and giving publicity to the world's cultural and artistic heritages, the Foreign Languages Press has produced this small album which introduces sites in China which have been recognized by UNESCO as being worthy of inclusion in its list of the common cultural and artistic wealth of mankind.

Luo Zhewen
Vice-President of China ICOMOS

Harmony between nature and human beings is the essence of traditional Chinese culture. Numerous examples can be found of the perfect combination of nature and culture in China's mountains and rivers. As of November 2003, the Chinese natural and cultural heritage sites approved by the UNESCO World Heritage Committee for inclusion on the World Heritage List included the Taishan, Huangshan and Wuyi mountains, which possess unparalleled scenery, long histories and abundant mountain-related culture and are therefore among the few heritage sites that are both cultural and natural. Huanglong, Jiuzhaigou, the Three Parallel Rivers and Wulingyuan have been included in the World Natural Heritage List because of their wonderful scenery, rare geological formations and unique topography. Mount Lushan has been included in the World Cultural Heritage List because of its delicate scenery and especially its cultural variety. These scenic heritage sites symbolize the intimate relationship between human beings and nature, with their graceful scenery and abundant culture enhancing each other's radiance and beauty.

❶ Mount Taishan

❷ Mount Huangshan

❸ Jiuzhaigou Valley Scenic and Historic Interest Area

❹ Huanglong Scenic and Historic Interest Area

❺ Wulingyuan Scenic and Historic Interest Area

❻ Lushan National Park

❼ Mount Wuyi

❽ The Three Parallel Rivers of Yunnan Protected Areas

Contents

Mount Taishan (UNESCO cultural and natural heritage site since 1987)

Mount Taishan, in central Shandong Province, is a mountain which occupies an important place in Chinese culture. Among the many sayings with Taishan as the theme is one which goes "As firm as Mount Taishan." The mountain was formed during the Archaeozoic era, approximately two billion years ago. Jade Emperor Peak (Yuhuangding), the main peak, soars 1,545 m above sea level, and visitors climb up here constantly to view the sunrise from the summit.

Rulers throughout Chinese history have bestowed honorific titles on Taishan, and several of them have worshipped on its peak. One of its titles is "Eastern Mountain, the first of the Five Great Mountains." Men of letters of all eras have visited Taishan, and left behind poems, essays and inscriptions praising it. Also, there are many Taoist temples and Buddhist monasteries on the mountain. At present, there are 22 ancient buildings and over 1,800 stone inscriptions on Mount Taishan, including the Diamond Sutra, carved during the Northern Qi Dynasty (550-577).

Bixia (Azure Cloud) Temple.

Confucius, the great Chinese philosopher and educator from the Spring and Autumn Period (770-476 BC), once climbed Mount Taishan. This is the place where he began his ascent. ▶

The 18 bends of Mount Taishan.

A ceremony to offer sacrifices to Heaven and Earth.

The highest of China's five most famous mountains.

Pine trees on Mount Taishan.

The Vajrachchedika-prajnaparamita-sutra (Diamond Sutra).

Pine trees on Mount Taishan.

Bixia (Azure Cloud) Temple.

"Inscriptions on Mount Taishan" engraved in 726 on Daguan (Grand View) Peak cliff and measuring 13.3 m high and 5.3 m wide.

A boxwood statue of the God of Longevity. This statue was placed on Mount Taishan, which implies a life longer than the mountain.

Copper statues in Bixia (Azure Cloud) Temple.

A copper statue in Bixia
Temple.

Tiandi (Heaven and
Earth) Square.

◄
Confucius is said to have once stood at this spot and looked towards his homeland, the State of Lu.

A Song Dynasty (960-1279) mural in the Tiankuang (Heavenly Blessing) Hall.

Mount Huangshan (UNESCO cultural and natural heritage site since 1990)

The 154-sq-km Mount Huangshan scenic area in southern Anhui Province contains over 400 natural views. There are 77 peaks of over 1,000 m around the Lianhua (Lotus) Peak, the highest point, 1,846 m above sea level. In addition, there are about 100 springs and pools. Mount Huangshan is noted for its steep cliffs, rugged pine trees, exotic rocks, "sea of clouds" and hot springs. With 83 percent of vegetation coverage, a stable ecological environment and 1,450 protophytes, it is a treasure-house of plant resources in southern China.

As a famous cultural mountain, Mount Huangshan has a long history, attracting numerous men of letters, celebrities and renowned scholars from ancient to modern times. There are over 20,000 poems in praise of it, nearly 100 extant ancient buildings, 200 stone inscriptions, and 36,000 stone steps on the 50,000 m of the ancient "rocky mountain path," connecting all the scenic spots.

Sunrise over Mount Huangshan.

Mount Huangshan shrouded in a sea of clouds.

"Buddha's halo."

"Paradise on Earth."

25

Peaks of Mount Huangshan.

Guest-Welcoming Pine.

A gracefully shaped centuries-old tree.

"Monkey watching the sea."

A white pine tree.

Mount Huang-shan covered with snow.

Sunset over Mount Huangshan.

Rocks on Mount Huangshan.

Jiuzhaigou Valley Scenic and Historic Interest Area (UNESCO natural heritage site since 1992)

The Jiuzhaigou Valley Scenic and Historic Interest Area is situated in Nanping County of the Aba Tibetan and Qiang Autonomous Region, Sichuan Province, with an area of 720 sq km. Mostly covered by forests and dotted by lakes and pools of various sizes, it has more than 2,000 varieties of higher plants, over 400 types of lower plants and 17 kinds of rare animals. Worshipped as a sacred mountain with holy springs, Jiuzhaigou is of extremely high scientific and aesthetic value.

The Changhai (Long Sea) Lake.

Jiuzhaigou in early autumn.

Nuorilang Waterfall.

The Peacock River.

The Five-Flower Lake.

The Rhinoceros Lake.

The Pearl Beach Waterfall.

Shuzheng Falls.

Huanglong Scenic and Historic Interest Area (UNESCO natural heritage site since 1992)

The Huanglong Scenic and Historic Interest Area is located in Songpan County of the Aba Tibetan and Qiang Autonomous Region, Sichuan Province, with an area of 700 sq km. It is over 3,000 m above sea level, surrounded by snowy peaks. With perfectly preserved geological structures, remnants of glaciation and the topographic features of river sources, it is world-renowned for its colorful ponds, glaciers, valleys and forests. It is also rich in animal and plant germ plasm resources.

A shining waterfall.

Pool edges formed by calcium
carbonate sediment.

51

The Five-colored Pool.

The Huanglong (Yellow Dragon) Temple.

Miniature landscape in water.

"The Stone Pagoda Stabilizing the sea."

Beautiful hills reflected in limpid pools.

Colorful pools.

Wulingyuan Scenic and Historic Interest Area (UNESCO natural heritage site since 1992)

The Wulingyuan Scenic and Historic Interest Area near Zhangjiajie City, Hunan Province, which has an area of 264 sq km and over 3,000 peaks, is called a place of "800 beautiful streams." The streams never stop flowing, even during periods of drought. The unique quartz-sandstone geology of Wulingyuan is rare both in China and the rest of the world. It has preserved the primitive features of the ancient plant communities of the Yangtze River valley, and the ancient ginkgo trees are called "living fossils." World-renowned for its grotesque peaks and stones, deep and secluded valleys, beautiful streams and karst caves, the Wulingyuan Scenic Spot is home to many items of scientific and tourism value.

Zhusun (Bamboo Shoot) Peak.

Mount Tianzi (Son of Heaven).

"Goddess Strewing Flowers."

Mount Tianzi (Son of Heaven).

Lushan National Park (UNESCO cultural heritage site since 1996)

Mount Lushan in northern Jiangxi Province, with an area of 302 sq km, features Quaternary glacier topography with rivers, lakes and peaks, and is known as a "geological park." Rich in biological resources, the mountain area boasts a complete ecological system.

In 391 Hui Yuan, a Buddhist leader, built Donglin (Eastern Grove) Temple here, which later became a Buddhist center for the whole of South China. A Taoist priest named Lu Xiujing established the Taoist Nantianshi School on the mountain in the fifth century, and Ma Zudao established the Linji and Weiyang sects of Taoism here during the Tang Dynasty (618-907). During the Ming (1368-1644)and Qing (1644-1911) dynasties, Islamic, Catholic and Protestant places of worship were established on Mount Lushan.

Hanpo (Embracing Poyang Lake) Pass.

A pine tree on Mount Lushan.

Huanglong (Yellow Dragon) Pool.

Xianren (Immortal's) Cave.

Sandie (Three-Step) Waterfall.

Xizhijian (Sunlight Ravine) Waterfall.

Xianzhang
(Immortal's
Palm) Rock.

Wulao (Five Old Men) Peak.

Bailu (White Deer) Cave.

73

74

An ancient work of calligraphy.

Shenyun (Divinely Blessed Fortune) Hall.

A stone carving of Master Ciyuan in Donglin (Eastern Grove) Temple.

Lake Huajing
(Flowery Path).

The tomb of Tao Yuanming (c. 376-427), a poet of the Eastern Jin Dynasty.

Mount Wuyi (UNESCO cultural and natural heritage site since 1999)

Mount Wuyi, on the boundary between Fujian and Jiangxi provinces, soars to a height of 2,118 m. The area is characterized by beautiful and magnificent views. A vast area of virgin forest high up on the mountain, with a rare stretch of Chinese hemlock trees, has been listed as a national nature reserve.

Mount Wuyi has long been sacred to Taoists, and the Taoist place of worship known as the Wuyi Palace has a history of over 1,000 years. Zhu Xi, philosopher and scholar of the Song Dynasty, lived and lectured here for more than 40 years. The numerous engravings of the Song, Yuan (1271-1368), Ming (1368-1644) and Qing (1644-1911) dynasties carved on the cliffs of the banks of the Nine-bend River (Jiuquxi), have important historic and artistic value. Of particular interest are the ancient boat-shaped coffins attached high up on the sides of cliffs.

The sixth bend.

Yunü (Jade Maiden) Peak.

Dawang (Great King) Peak.

Cloud Sea.

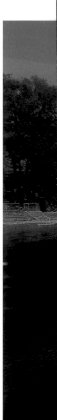

Tourists climbing Tianyou (Heavenly Tour) Peak.

The tour along the Nine-Bends Stream begins at Xingcun (Star Village) and follows the flow of the stream.

The meadow grassland of Mount Huanggang.

Rough gentian from high up the mountain.

The Three Parallel Rivers of Yunnan Protected Areas (UNESCO natural heritage site since 2003)

The Three Parallel Rivers natural scenic area covers an area of 41,000 sq km and consists of the Nujiang, Lancang and Jinsha rivers and the mountains at their basins. It is located in the rift valley of the Hengduan Mountains, which are part of the southern extension of the Qinghai-Tibet Plateau. Being a place where the three geographical regions of East Asia, South Asia and the Qinghai-Tibet Plateau meet, alpine landforms and their development can be seen, making it an unusual area. It is also one of the world's richest areas for species of fauna and flora. Home to 16 nationalities, it is also an unusual area because so many different nationalities, languages, religions and customs coexist there.

The Meli Snow Mountain.
The mountain ridge is covered with snow all year round. Thirteen of the peaks rise to more than 6,000 m above sea level. Of these, Kagebo Peak is the highest in Yunnan Province, with groups of pilgrims traveling great distances to visit it at the end of autumn and beginning of winter each year.

The first bend of the Yangtze River.

Zimei (Sisters) Pool at Mount Laojun.

Hutiao (Leaping Tiger) Gorge.

Lake Bita (Green Jade Pagoda).

图书在版编目（CIP）数据

自然与文化／罗哲文主编.
－北京：外文出版社，2003.12
（中国的世界遗产）

ISBN 7-119-03401-4

Ⅰ. 自... Ⅱ. 罗... Ⅲ.①名胜古迹－简介－中国－英文
②文化遗址－简介－中国－英文 Ⅳ. K928.7

中国版本图书馆 CIP 数据核字（2003）第 066635 号

策　　划	肖晓明
责任编辑	杨春燕
英文翻译	张韶宁
英文审定	郁苓
图片提供	兰佩瑾　孙永学　孙志江　孙树明　刘春根
	杜泽泉　罗哲文　茹遂初　高明义　高纯瑞
版式设计	蔡荣
印刷监制	张国祥

外文出版社网址：
　http://www.flp.com.cn
外文出版社电子信箱：
　info@flp.com.cn
　sales@flp.com.cn

中国的世界遗产

自然与文化

罗哲文　主编

*

© 外文出版社
外文出版社出版
（中国北京百万庄大街 24 号）
邮政编码　100037
北京大容彩色印刷有限公司印制
中国国际图书贸易总公司发行
（中国北京车公庄西路 35 号）
北京邮政信箱第 399 号　邮政编码　100044
2004 年(小 24 开)第 1 版
2004 年第 1 版第 1 次印刷
（英）
ISBN 7-119-03401-4/J · 1656(外)
02800(平)
85-E-566 P